CW01044053

Poems for Home schoolers

A collection of relatable rhymes & poems for home educated children and their parents.

Plus 'Write Your Own' poetry prompts to help you share your own experiences through poetry.

SASKIA CRAWLEY

About the writer

Saskia Crawley is a writer and home educating mum of three from Cheltenham, Gloucestershire in the UK. Having realised how many children's poetry anthologies include school references, 'Poems for Homeschoolers' was written so home educated families can now experience their daily life through poetic form too!

For more creative works celebrating home education visit:
http://tiny.cc/thenoschoolerssociety

To get in touch with Saskia (including to share any poems inspired by the prompts inside this book) email: thenoschoolerssociety@gmail.com

Dedication

To my children and husband.
What a gift it is to share so many ordinary days
with such extraordinary people

Contents

Late start

At school they start at 9am,

while I'm tucked up in bed.

I think I'll get my rest today,

and learn tonight instead.

My teacher

My teacher lets me jump about,

My teacher lets me whistle.

My teacher lets me snack in class,

My teacher lets me giggle.

My teacher lets me ask a lot,

My teacher lets me hum.

My teacher lets me chat non-stop,

My teacher is my mum.

Bedtime lessons

Some of my best learning,

happens right before bed.

When everything is quiet,

but the questions in my head.

Sleepy conversations.

Things I want to know.

"Can you look it up, please?"

That's how my bedtimes go.

Creativity

The thing I love most about home education,

is all the time free to spend on creation.

Animations, drawings, expressive art.

Music, sculpture, taking things apart.

Designing, refining, planning. and prep.

There's so much learning in every step.

Homeschool hair

Long hair.

Wild hair.

Hair that can't be tamed.

Bright hair.

Fierce hair.

Hair that won't be shamed.

Weird hair.

Silly hair.

Hair that breaks the rules.

Shaved hair.

Brave hair.

Hair too cool for school.

I wonder

I wonder what we're doing today,

I wonder where we'll go,

I wonder what I'll learn today,

There's so much I want to know...

I wonder what I'll make today,

I wonder what I'll play,

I wonder what I'll learn today,

It's up to me! Hooray!

WRITE YOUR OWN:

Anaphora

'I wonder' is an Anaphora poem, a poem that uses the repetition of phrases or words at the start of each line. It's a great way to emphasise meaning, add rhythm, and help your reader/listener reflect.

Pick a phrase or word and have a go at writing your own Anaphora poem. What can you come up with?

Doing it my way

I don't have a classroom,

I don't have a desk.

I don't have a headteacher,

who thinks they know best.

The world is my oyster,

my home is my base.

I learn when I want to,

life isn't a race.

This week's timetable

A little bit of cooking,

a lot of time outside.

An hour or three experimenting,

five spent on the slide.

An afternoon of Lego,

a morning to animate.

A library visit, a cafe stop,

a museum playdate.

A day spent in our PJs,

an evening staying up.

Life is our education,

and learning's what we love.

Socialising

"But how will they socialise?"

I hear grownups say...

"They'll never see people!"

They frown in dismay.

If only they knew, while projecting their strife,

who I will engage with while out doing life.

A postman.

A plumber.

5 kids at the park.

A bus driver.

Librarian.

My uncle and aunt.

A doctor.

A cashier.

3 teachers, online.

A waiter.

My siblings...

I'm going to be fine!

A homeschool interrogation

"Is your mum a 'proper' teacher?"

"Do you have to sit exams?"

"Do you have to stay at home all day?"

"Do you still put up your hand?"

"Do you miss out on playtime?"

"Don't you want to do PE?"

"Do you have a desk to work from?"

"Is there 'homework' after tea?"

"Do you wish you had more friends though?"

"Do you think you'll fall behind?"

"Are you fed up of your family?"

"Is school ever on your mind?"

                                    "No..."

"Oh."

WRITE YOUR OWN:

Dialogue

A dialogue poem reflects speech between two or more people, representing different perspectives on a theme or topic. 'A homeschool interrogation' features many different questioning voices, with one response to answer them all towards the end. What conversations can you express through poetry? Give it a go!

Things homeschoolers often say

"Will you come and look at this?"

"Did you know…"

"Can I show you what I'm working on?"

"Where shall we go?"

"I've got a great idea!"

"How do you spell…"

"Let's research it then."

"Can we do that today as well?"

Playground kings

My brother and I, are playground kings.

We climb up the slides,

and go wild on the swings.

We race 'round in circles,

we imagine,

we chase.

In school time hours,

we rule the whole place!

When things don't go to plan

We wake up late.

Everyone is grumpy.

Nobody wants to leave the house.

So we won't.

We'll watch TV instead,

and try again tomorrow.

Endless questions

How?

Where?

When?

Answers to find.

Who?

What?

Which?

Questions all the time.

L.e.a.r.n

Let your curiosity lead you,

each pondering as important as the last.

Are there any questions on your mind?

Rarely do we stop asking.

Now is the time to find answers!

WRITE YOUR OWN:

Acrostic

An Acrostic poem is where when the first letter of each line is read vertically it spells out a chosen word. Look at 'L.e.a.r.n' to see this in action, then pick a word to try and give it a go yourself.

Screentime skills

Coding.

    Poetry.

        Writing plays.

           Gamebuilding.

               Strategizing.

                    Documentaries.

              Emailing.

          Researching.

              Illustration.

      Editing.

          Stop motion.

              Graphics creation.

                    Reading.

              Analysing.

          Checking stats.

I learn loads from my screentime, as a matter of fact.

Just being

I feel a bit sad, for the kids at school,

sitting as they're told, following the rules.

When I'm at home, I just sort of... be,

getting on with my day, left to be me.

I try out ideas, I read, I draw.

I have tonnes of questions I'm free to explore.

And if I get bored, well, that's OK,

I just stop and spend time in a different way.

An important lesson

When projects go wrong, it hurts my head.

I want to give up, but I try again instead.

Wait and see

People keep asking me, what I "want to be?"

I'm not really sure yet... can I wait and see?

WRITE YOUR OWN:

Rhyming Couplets

'An important lesson' and 'Wait and see' are simple rhyming couplet poems. Two lines that rhyme. A couplet can be used on its own to express an idea, or as part of a longer poem. Can you write your own rhyming couplet?

Always learning

I learn from YouTube,

I learn from books,

I learn from magazines,

I learn when I cook,

I learn in the supermarket,

I learn at the park,

I learn in the forest,

I learn when it's dark,

I learn when I Google,

I learn when I run,

I learn watching Netflix,

I learn having fun,

I learn playing board games,

I learn when I draw,

I learn from nature,

I learn when I'm bored,

I learn in a gallery,

I learn from my friends,

I learn when I want to,

It just never ends.

What you'll learn from board games

Multiplication.

Addition.

Subtraction.

Communication.

Emotional reactions.

Creativity.

History.

Geography.

Art.

Consequences.

Strategy.

Losing graciously.

Or not.

Everyday messes

An egg in vinegar sat on the mantel.

A tabletop covered in Lego builds.

Twenty sheets of half-used paper.

Socks in odd places.

Leggings strewn across the floor.

A raisin or two, escaped from their box.

Pens without lids.

Abandoned workbooks.

A crumpled list of spellings.

Plenty of cardboard, ready for the taking.

Incomplete

Sometimes I change my mind.

Half-finished stories.

Workbooks left blank.

Puzzles incomplete.

Sometimes I find more interesting things to do.

Maybe I'll come back to them,

Maybe I -

WRITE YOUR OWN:

Using punctuation

The way you use punctuation in your poetry can have a powerful way of changing the meter (the rhythmic pattern), emphasis, or meaning. Have you noticed how the dash at the end of 'Incomplete' suggests the poem itself is unfinished? Can you write a poem of your own that uses punctuation to further emphasise your ideas?

Our subscription box

Every now and again, it drops through our door.

Ting! Thud.

It lands.

Mum walks over and picks up the slim, purple cardboard box.

It looks familiar, but it's never good to get your hopes up. Just in case.

She smiles in our direction and gently shakes the box in the air, so its insides jingle.

Yes! An afternoon's excitement gripped within her hands.

But what experiments lurk inside?

She turns and sneaks the box onto our bookshelf. Until tomorrow.

Blanket fort

Every homeschool home has had a blanket fort or two,

the bestest place to hide out when you've got a lot to do.

First, I'll do a workbook, then read a magazine. Then watch a documentary on the places that I've been.

When dinner time is looming, and I'm still sat in my nook. My mum can bring a picnic, and our favourite chapter book!

And then, I'll grab my cuddlies, and a battery-powered light - it really is so cosy...

I'll sleep in here! Alright?

The wriggler

I really don't like sitting still.

It makes me feel practically ill.

If I were in school, I'd break all the rules,

from wiggling and wriggling at will.

Limerick

'The wriggler' is a limerick. Limericks use a five-line structure and an AABBA rhyme scheme. Meaning the 1st, 2nd & 5th lines have the same rhythm and rhyme as each other, and the 3rd & 4th lines have the same rhythm and rhyme as each other.

Limericks are usually used to give a humorous description or tell a short story. What experience can you describe, or story can you tell, through a limerick?

The Zoom class

We click through on our invite,

turn the sound right up.

Tilt the screen a little, is it bright enough?

The host is joining.

Our faces glow.

A hundred other children tuning in from home.

The screen is divided,

an ocean of wild.

Jumping, wiggling,

silliness and smiles.

The teacher begins next,

some wave hello.

A reminder of the class rules

and away we go!

We listen for a little, then take a turn ourselves.

Cut, stick, doodle,

grab resources off the shelves.

Press to raise our hand now.

Show off what we've made.

Another session wrapped up,

and then it's back to play.

On the sofa

It sits, inviting.

A perfect mix of squashy and firm.

Waiting for me.

Waiting for me.

I wriggle my toes and wrinkle my nose,

then plant myself head first,

legs shooting out behind me.

Bosh.

I turn, twisting now on to my back.

A grin, a giggle, and then PING.

I sit myself back up. Bottom firmly planted.

Knees up beneath my chin.

I wriggle my toes again and stretch one arm out to
reach my favourite blanket.

Snuggled, cuddled.

I sit, comfortable.

The perfect place to start the day.

Perhaps I'll grab a book.

Perhaps I'll grab the TV remote.

Perhaps I'll do nothing but sit here, knowing I have a new day ahead, and plenty of time to spend here, in my favourite spot.

On the sofa.

The library

Can you believe there's a place you can go,

to get books for free, and read back at home.

Shelves upon shelves, packed with new worlds,

places to imagine, adventures to unfurl...

The only downside, of this magical place,

It's so hard to choose which stories to take!

Free verse

Free verse poetry has no strict rules. Meaning there's no strict meter (rhythm pattern) or rhyme scheme. Free verse poems often follow the natural patterns of speech. This gives you lots of freedom to share your ideas and express yourself. Reflect on your day-to-day life and see if you can share an experience through free verse!

Blanket fort

Every homeschool home has had a blanket fort or two,

the bestest place to hide out when you've got a lot to do.

First, I'll do a workbook, then read a magazine. Then watch a documentary on the places that I've been.

When dinner time is looming, and I'm still sat in my nook. My mum can bring a picnic, and our favourite chapter book!

And then, I'll grab my cuddlies, and a battery-powered light - it really is so cosy...

I'll sleep in here! Alright?

Learning to read without phonics books

Subtitles,

video games,

messages,

jokes.

Brochures,

instructions,

labels,

remotes.

Signposts,

manuals,

tickets,

lists.

Magazines,

packaging...

You get the gist.

Craft supplies

One hundred felt tips, some without lids.

A bottle of PVA, five sticks of Pritt.

Pompoms, stickers, feathers, chalk,

a collection of conkers picked up on a walk.

Plasticine, sequins, oil pastels too,

paper (all colours), plastic (see through).

Tissue, cotton, stencils, card,

plenty of pencils (soft lead and hard).

Labels, envelopes, erasers, clay,

Newspaper cuttings we can't throw away.

And last but not least, the Googly eyes...

You can tell a home edder, by their craft supplies.

A selection of places we gather

Cafés,

soft play,

church halls.

Woodland,

galleries,

swimming pools.

Beach fronts,

libraries,

beauty spots.

Playgrounds,

back yards,

allotment plots.

WRITE YOUR OWN:

Expressive lists

Rhyming lists can be a fun way to make a point and show others what's important to you. Can you write a poetic list to describe something about your life? Perhaps to describe your toy collection, your favourite animals, or the games you like to play?

No exams here

Schools want to test me.

There will be no exams here.

Life has enough trials.

An invitation

It's time to create.

Blank paper, boldly calls me.

What beauty awaits?

WRITE YOUR OWN:

Haikus

'No exams here' and 'An invitation' are both Haikus. A Haiku is a Japanese poem made up of 3 lines and 17 syllables. The first line is 5 syllables, the second line is 7, and the final line is 5 syllables long. Following the rules of a Haiku can be a lot of fun, like doing a puzzle! Can you write your own?

The unschooling parent

Chief of supervision.

Patience, a must.

Long-term vision.

Bags of trust.

Snacktime

Oh, to have our days punctuated by such predictable delight.

A chance to rest, connect, and munch on yummies that we like.

Once in the morning, again around three,

essential refreshments to keep us going until tea.

WRITE YOUR OWN:

Ode

An ode is a lyrical poem (a poem that shares the writer's emotions) celebrating a person, place, event or thing. 'Snacktime' is an ode to a great part of the day! What person, place, event or thing can you celebrate with a poem?

My morning art session

Stick. Rip.

Chop, cut, glue.

Colour, colour,

red, yellow, blue.

Splash. Stamp.

Print, squash, fold.

Blend, mix,

brown, black, gold.

Shade, outline,

sculpt, sculpt, scrunch.

Paper. Cardboard.

Collage.

Lunch.

The printer

Our printers not working,

it's quite on the blink.

Which is very frustrating,

there's plenty of ink!

The display shows an error,

it just won't connect.

It's this printer oddness,

we've come to expect.

Afters hours of trying,

with all of our might,

it'll start without warning,

and gives us a fright!

Homeschool rules

I can wear what I want.

I can sleep when I'm tired.

I can pee when I need to,

no permission required.

I can eat when I'm hungry,

and drink when I need.

It's simple stuff really,

at home I am free.